MARIJUANA

Growing marijuana indoor

by

Daan Joie

this publication is strictly prohibited and any storage of this document is not allowed unless with

written permission from the publisher. All rights reserved.

Daan Joie |

The information herein is offered for informational purposes solely and is universal as so. The presentation of the information is without the contract or any type of guarantee assurance.

The trademarks that are used are without any consent, and the publication of the trademark is without permission or backing by the trademark owner. All trademarks and brands within this book are for clarifying purposes only and are the owned by the owners themselves, not affiliated with this document.

Contents

Daan Joie |

<u>Introduction</u>

Marijuana is the common name for the psychoactive genetic variation of the cannabis sativa plant. Used for over a thousand years in central Asia, it has been smoked for over a century in America, gaining wide usage during the counterculture 1960's, and ever since then has been the most widely used illicit drug in America.

The strength and potency have increased greatly through advances in genetic manipulation and growing conditions (hydroponics), and today's marijuana can be as much as 15 times stronger than the drug of the 1960's and 70's. This dramatic increase in potency has nullified much of our understanding of the effects of the drug, and any research done on the intoxication and damages of the smoked drug prior to about a decade ago do not accurately reflect the realities of today's marijuana.

AN OVERVIEW

The main active ingredient is Delta-9-Tetrahydrocannabinol (THC), which binds to the CB1 receptors of our cannibanoid systems in the brain and throughout the body. It is the THC that gets you high, and it is the THC content that has been steadily increasing over the past decades.

Although THC is the primary intoxicating active substance, there are an additional 400 active or semi active substance present in varying degrees in different strains of marijuana. Of these 400 active substances, few have been clinically explored, and although they do certainly exert some psychotropic influence, researchers do not fully understand what this influence may be. Smokers will realize that variations in the expression of these different molecules cause the high from different types of marijuana to be ☐uite different.

These 400 active molecules also seem important for the drugs efficacy as a medication, and although scientists have synthesized THC in a pill form, the absence of this comprehensive mix of other chemicals seems to decrease the usefulness of this synthesized medication. Medical marijuana remains a controversial topic, even within the medical community, and although a great many public health groups have called for its usage, the AMA and the FDA most notably oppose its approval.

Marijuana has been in existence for over decades, and it has its own benefits and likewise does it comes with disadvatages but despite that we have alot of popular people who seems to believe marijuana does something better. Therefore, to be more precise.

Many countries have decriminalized the possession of small quantities of cannabis;

Some states in the US allow use of medical cannabis in state, territorial, Indian reservation, and Federal district laws, although the use is illegal by federal law. Federal agencies claim that federal law comes first.

As of 2015, Bangladesh, Cambodia, Canada, Chile, Colombia, the Czech Republic, India, Jamaica, Mexico, Portugal, Spain, Uruguay, Germany, the Netherlands, some U.S. states, Native American Indian reservations, and cities as well as some territories of Australia have the least restrictive cannabis laws while China, Egypt, France, Indonesia, Japan, Malaysia, Nigeria, Norway, the Philippines, Poland, Saudi Arabia, Singapore,

South Korea, Thailand, Turkey, Ukraine, the United Arab Emirates and Vietnam have the strictest cannabis laws.

What Happens When You Smoke Marijuana?

After smoking, the THC and other active chemicals are absorbed through the lungs and passed quickly into the bloodstream; and within about a minute the effects of the THC start to be felt. The intensity of the high will continue to increase for about 20 minutes, before plateauing and gradually leveling off over about 2 hours.

When you smoke, the THC absorbed into the bloodstream passes into the brain and attaches itself to receptors in the endo cannibanoid system, a system found throughout many higher order parts of the brain. Once these receptors in the brain are stimulated by THC, the user begins to experience changes in sensory perception, in time perception, in concentration and cognitive abilities, in coordination, and in appetite. The endo cannibanoid system is linked to the pleasure system of the brain, and when activated it causes a dopaminergic reaction, allowing for pleasurable and relaxed sensations in addition to these other sensory alterations. For the vast majority of users, marijuana provokes a relaxed and enjoyable high that lasts for a couple of hours, and leaves little obvious harm in its wake.

When marijuana is taken in very large doses, it can cause hallucinogenic reactions. Some users will also experience negative reactions to the drug, such as anxiety, paranoia and panic, and a full 30% of users who eventually give up the drug report that they do so as a result of these experienced negative sensations.

Growing marijuana indoors

Growing marijuana indoors is fast becoming an American Pastime. The reasons are varied. With the increased interest and experimentation in houseplant cultivation, it was inevitable that people would apply their knowledge of plant care to growing marijuana. Many of those who occasionally like to light up a joint may find it difficult to locate a source or are hesitant to deal with a perhaps unsavory element of society in procuring their grass. There is, of course, the criminal aspect of buying or selling grass; Growing marijuana is **just as illegal as buying, selling, or smoking** it, but growing is something you can do in the privacy of your own home without having to deal with someone you don't know or trust. The best reason for growing your own is the enjoyment you will get out of watching those tiny little seeds you picked out of you stash sprout and become some of the most lovely and lush of all house plants.

ANYONE CAN DO IT

IN 4 STEPS

Even if you haven't had any prior experience with growing plants in your home, you can have a successful crop of marijuana by following the simple directions in this pamphlet. If you have had problems in the past with marijuana cultivation, you may find the solutions in the following chapters. Growing a marijuana plant involves four basic steps:

1. Get the seeds. If you don't already have some, you can ask your friends to save you seeds out of any good grass they may come across. You'll find that lots of people already have a seed collection of some sort and are willing to part with a few prime seeds in exchange for some of the finished product.

2. Germinate the seeds. You can simply drop a seed into moist soil, but by germinating the seeds first you can be sure that the seed will indeed produce a plant. To germinate seeds, place a group of them between about six moist paper towels, or in the pores of a moist sponge. Leave the towels or sponge moist but not soaking wet. Some seeds will germinate in 24 hours while others may take several days or even a week.

3. Plant the sprouts. As soon as the seed cracks open and begin to sprout, place it on some moist soil and sprinkle a little soil over the top of it.

4. Supply the plants with light. Fluorescent lights are the best. Hang the lights with two inches of the soil and after the plants appear above the ground, continue to keep the lights with two inches of the plants. It is as easy as that. If you follow those four steps you will grow a marijuana plant. To ensure

prime ☐uality and the highest yield in the shortest time period, however, a few details are necessary.

SOIL

Your prime concern, after choosing high quality seeds, is the soil. Use the best soil you can get. Scrimping on the soil doesn't pay off in the long run. If you use non-sterilized soil you will almost certainly find parasites in it, probably after it is too late to transplant your marijuana. You can find excellent soil for sale at your local plant shop or nursery, K-Mart, Wal-Mart, and even some grocery stores. The soil you use should have these properties for the best possible results:

1. It should drain well. That is, it should have some sand in it and also some sponge rock or pearlite.

2. The pH should be between 6.5 and 7.5 since marijuana does not do well in acidic soil. High

acidity in soil encourages the plant to be predominantly male, an undesirable trait.

3. The soil should also contain humus for retaining moisture and nutrients. If you want to make your own soil mixture, you can use this recipe: Mix two parts moss with one part sand and one part pearlite or sponge rock to each four gallons of soil. Test your soil for pH with litmus paper or with a soil testing kit available at most plant stores. To raise the pH of the soil, add ½ lb. lime to 1 cubic foot of soil to raise the pH one point. If you absolutely insist on using dirt you dug up from your driveway, you must sterilize it by baking it in your oven for about an hour at 250 degrees. Be sure to moisten it thoroughly first and also prepare yourself for a rapid evacuation of your kitchen because that hot soil is going to stink. Now add to the mixture about one tablespoon of fertilizer (like Rapid-Gro) per gallon of soil and blend it in thoroughly. Better yet,

just skip the whole process and spend a couple bucks on some soil.

CONTAINERS

After you have prepared your soil, you will have to come up with some kind of container to plant in. The container should be sterilized as well, especially if they have been used previously for growing other plants. The size of the container has a great deal to do with the rate of growth and overall size of the plant. You should plan on transplanting your plant not more than one time, since the process of transplanting can be a shock to the plant and it will have to undergo a recovery period in which growth is slowed or even stopped for a short while. The first container you use should be no larger than six inches in diameter and can be made of clay or plastic. To transplant, simply prepare the larger pot by filling it with soil and scooping out a little hole about the size of the smaller pot that the plant is in. Turn the plant upside down, pot and all, and tap the rim of the pot sharply on a counter or the edge of the sink. The soil and root ball should come out of the pot cleanly with the soil retaining the shape of the pot and with no disturbances to the root ball. Another method that can bypass the transplanting problem is using a Jiffy-Pot.

Jiffy pots are made of compressed peat moss and can be planted right into moist soil where they decompose and allow the passage of the root system through their walls. The second container should have a volume of at least three gallons. Marijuana doesn't like to have its roots bound or cramped for space, so always be sure that the container you use will be deep enough for your plant's root system. It is very difficult to transplant a five-foot marijuana tree, so plan ahead. It is going to get bigger. The small plants should be ready to transplant into their permanent homes in about two weeks. Keep a close watch on them after the first week or so and avoid root binding at all costs since the plants never seem to do as well once they have been stunted by the cramping of their roots.

FERTILIZER

Marijuana likes lots of food, but you can do damage to the plants if you are too zealous. Some fertilizers can burn a plant and damage its roots if used in to high a concentration. Most commercial soil will have enough nutrients in it to sustain the plant for about three weeks of growth so you don't need to worry about feeding your plant until the end of the third week. The most important thing to remember is to introduce the fertilizer concentration to the plant gradually. Start with a fairly diluted fertilizer solution and gradually increase the dosage. There are several good marijuana fertilizers on the commercial market, two of which are Rapid-Gro and Eco-Grow. Rapid-Gro has had widespread use in marijuana cultivation and is available in most parts of the United States. Eco-Grow is also especially good for marijuana since it contains an ingredient that keeps the soil from becoming acid. Most fertilizers cause a pH change in the soil. Adding fertilizer to the soil almost always results in a more acidic pH. As time goes on, the amount of salts produced by the breakdown of fertilizers in the soil causes the soil to become increasingly acidic and eventually the concentration of these salts in the soil will stunt the plant and cause browning out of the foliage. Also, as the plant gets older its roots become less effective in bringing food to the leaves. To avoid the accumulation of these salts in your soil and to ensure that your plant is getting all of the food it needs you can begin leaf feeding your plant at the age of about 1.5 months. Dissolve the fertilizer in worm water and spray the mixture directly onto the foliage. The leaves absorb the fertilizer into their veins. If you want to continue to put fertilizer into the soil as well as leaf feeding, be sure not to overdose your plants.

Remember to increase the amount of food your plant receives gradually. Marijuana seems to be able to take as much fertilizer as you want to give it as long as it is introduced over a period of time. During the first three months or so, fertilize your plants every few days. As the rate of foliage growth slows down in the plant's preparation for blooming and seed production, the fertilizer intake of the plant should be slowed down as well. Never fertilize the plant just before you are going to harvest it since the fertilizer will encourage foliage production and slow down resin production. A word here about the most organic of fertilizers: worm castings. As you may know, worms are raised commercially for sale to gardeners. The breeders put the worms in organic compost mixtures and while the worms are reproducing they eat the organic matter and expel some of the best marijuana food around. After the worms have eaten all the organic matter in the compost, they are removed and sold and the remains are then sold as worm castings. These castings are so rich that you can grow marijuana in straight worm castings. This isn't really necessary however, and it is somewhat impractical since the castings are very expensive. If you can afford them you can, however, blend them in with your soil and they will make a very good organic fertilizer.

LIGHT

Without light, the plants cannot grow. In the countries in which marijuana grows best, the sun is the source of light. The amount of light and the length of the growing season in these countries result in huge tree-like plants. In most parts of North America, however, the sun is not generally intense enough for long enough periods of time to produce the same size and quality of plants that grow with ease in Latin America and other tropical countries. The answer to the problem of lack of sun, especially in the winter months, shortness of the growing season and other problems is to grow indoors under simulated conditions. The rule of thumb seems to be the more light, the better. In one experiment we know of, eight eight-foot VHO Gro-Lux fixtures were used over eight plants. The plants grew at an astonishing rate. The lights had to be raised every day. There are many types of artificial light and all of them do different things to your plants. The common incandescent light bulb emits some of the fre☐uencies of light the plant can use, but it also emits a high percentage of far-red and infrared light, which cause the plant to concentrate its growth on the stem. This results in the plant stretching toward the light bulb until it becomes so tall and spindly that it just weakly topples over. There are several brands of bulb type.

One is the incandescent plant spotlight, which emits higher amounts of red and blue light than the common light bulb. It is an improvement, but has it

Daan Joie |

drawbacks. it is hot, for example, and cannot be placed close to the plants. Conse□uently, the plant has to stretch upwards again and is in danger of becoming elongated and falling over. The red bands of light seem to encourage stem growth, which is not desirable in growing marijuana. The idea is to encourage foliage growth for obvious reasons. Gro-Lux lights are probably the most common fluorescent plant lights. In our experience with them, they have proven themselves to be extremely effective. They range in size from one to eight feet in length so you can set up a growing room in a closet or a warehouse. There are two types of Gro-Lux lights: The standard and the wide spectrum. They can be used in conjunction with on another, but the wide spectrum lights are not sufficient on their own. The wide spectrum lights were designed as a supplementary light source and are cheaper than the standard lights. Wide spectrum lights emit the same bands of light as the standard but the standard emits higher concentrations of red and blue bands that the plants need to grow.

The wide spectrum lights also emit infrared, the effect of which on stem growth we have already discussed. If you are planning to grow on a large scale, you might be interested to know that the regular fluorescent lamps and fixtures, the type that are used in commercial lighting, work well when used along with standard Gro-Lux lights. These commercial lights are called cool whites, and are the cheapest of the fluorescent lights we have mentioned. They emit as much blue light as the Gro-Lux standards and the blue light is what the plants use in foliage growth.

TEMPERATURE AND HUMIDITY

The ideal temperature for the light hours is 68 to 78 degrees Fahrenheit and for the dark hours there should be about a 15-degree drop in temperature. The growing room should be relatively dry if possible. What you want is a resinous coating on the leaves and to get the plant to do this, you must convince it that it needs the resinous coating on its leaves to protect itself from drying out. In an extremely humid room, the plants develop wide leaves and do not produce as much resin. You must take care not to let the temperature in a dry room become too hot, however, since the plant cannot assimilate water fast enough through its roots and its foliage will begin to brown out.

VENTILATION

Proper ventilation in your growing room is fairly important. The more plants you have in one room, the more important good ventilation becomes. Plants breathe through their leaves. The also rid themselves of poisons through their leaves. If proper ventilation is not maintained, the pores of the leaves will become clogged and the leaves will die. If there is a free movement of air, the poisons can evaporate off the leaves and the plant can breathe and remain healthy.

In a small closet where there are only a few plants you can probably create enough air circulation just by opening the door to look at them. Although it is possible to grow healthy looking plants in poorly ventilated rooms, they would be larger and healthier if they had a fresh supply of air coming in. If you spend a lot of time in your growing room, your plants will grow better because they will be using the carbon dioxide that you are exhaling around them. It is sometimes quite difficult to get a fresh supply of air in to your growing room because your room is usually hidden away in a secret corner of your house, possibly in the attic or basement. In this case, a fan will create some movement of air. It will also stimulate your plants into growing a healthier and sturdier stalk. Often times in an indoor environment, the stems of plants fail to become rigid because they don't have to cope with elements of wind and rain. To a degree, though, this is an advantage because the plant puts most of its energy into producing leaves and resin instead of stems.

DEHUMIDIFYING YOUR GROWING ROOM

Cannabis that grows in a hot, dry climate will have narrower leaves than cannabis grown in a humid atmosphere. The reason is that in a dry atmosphere the plants can respire easier because the moisture on the leaves evaporates faster. In a humid atmosphere, the moisture cannot evaporate as fast. Consequently, the leaves have to be broader with more surface area in order to expel the wastes that the plant put out. Since the broad leaves produce less resin per leaf than the narrow there will be more resin in an ounce of narrow leaves than in one ounce of broad leaves.

There may be more leaf mass in the broader leafed plants, but most people are growing their own for quality rather than quantity. Since the resin in the marijuana plant serves the purpose of keeping the leaves from drying out, there is more apt to be a lot of resin produced in a dry room than in a humid one. In the Sears catalog, dehumidifiers cost around $100.00 and are therefore a bit impractical for the "hobby grower."

WATERING

If you live near a clear mountain stream, you can skip this bit on the quality of water. Most of us are supplied water by the city and some cities add more chemicals to the water than others. They all add chlorine, however, in varying quantities. Humans over the years have learned to either get rid of it somehow or to live with it, but your marijuana plants won't have time to acquire a taste for it so you had better see that they don't have to. Chlorine will evaporate if you let the water stand for 24 hours in an open container. Letting the water stand for a day or two will serve a dual purpose: The water will come to room temperature during that period of time and you can avoid the nasty shock your plants suffer when you drench them with cold water. Always water with room temperature to lukewarm water.

If your water has an excessive amount of chlorine in it, you may want to get some anti- chlorine drops at the local fish or pet store. The most important thing about watering is to do it thoroughly. You can water a plant in a threegallon container with as much as three quarts of water. The idea is to get the soil evenly moist all the way to the bottom of the pot. If you use a little water, even if you do it often, it seeps just a short way down into the soil and any roots below the moist soil will start to turn upwards toward the water. The second most important thing about watering is to see to it that the pot has good drainage. There should be some holes in the bottom so that any excess water will run out. If the pot won't drain, the excess water will accumulate in a pocket and rot the roots of the plant or simply make the soil sour or mildew. The soil, as we said earlier, must allow the water to drain evenly through it and must not become hard or packed. If you have made sure that the soil contains sand and pearlite, you shouldn't have drainage problems. To discover when to water, feel the soil with your finger. if you feel moisture in the soil, you can wait a day or two to water. The soil near the top of the pot is always drier than the soil further down. You can drown your plant just as easily as you can let it get too dry and it is more likely to survive a dry spell than it is to survive a torrential flood. Water the plants well when you water and don't water them at all when they don't need it.

Daan Joie |

PRUNING

We have found that pruning is not always necessary. The reason one does it in the first place is to encourage secondary growth and to allow light to reach the immature leaves. Some strands of grass just naturally grow thick and bushy and if they are not clipped the sap moves in an uninterrupted flow right to the top of the plant where it produces flowers that are thick with resin. On the other hand, if your plants appear tall and spindly for their age at three weeks, they probably require a little trimming to ensure a nice full leafy plant. At three weeks of age your plant should have at least two sets of branches or four leaf clusters and a top. To prune the plant, simply slice the top off just about the place where two branches oppose each other. Use a razor blade in a straight cut. If you want to, you can root the top in some water and when the roots appear, plant the top in moist soil and it should grow into another plant. If you are going to root the top you should cut the end again, this time with a diagonal cut so as to expose more surface to the water or rooting solution. The advantage to taking cuttings from your plant is that it produces more tops. The tops have the resin, and that's the name of the game. Every time you cut off a top, the plant seeds out two more top branches at the base of the existing branches. Pruning also encourages the branches underneath to grow faster than they normally would without the top having been cut.

HARVESTING AND CURING

Well, now that you've grown your marijuana, you will want to cur it properly so that it smokes clean and won't bite. You can avoid that "homegrown" taste of chlorophyll that sometimes makes one's fillings taste like they might be dissolving. We know of several methods of curing the marijuana so that it will have a mild flavor and a mellow rather than harsh smoke.

First, pull the plant up roots and all and hang it upside down for 24 hours. Then put each plant in a paper grocery bag with the top open for three or four days or until the leaves feels dry to the touch. Now strip the leaves off the stem and put them in a glass jar with a lid. Don't pack the leaves in tightly, you want air to reach all the leaves. The main danger in the curing process is mold. If the leaves are too damp when you put them into the jar, they will mold and since the mold will destroy the resins, mold will ruin your marijuana. You should check the jars every day by smelling them and if you smell an acrid aroma take the weed out of the jar and spread it out on newspaper so that it can dry quickly. Another method is to uproot the plants and hang them upside down. You get some burlap bags damp and slip them up over the plants. Keep the bags damp and leave them in the sun for at least a week. Now put the plants in a paper bag for a few days until the weed is dry enough to smoke. Like many fine things in life, marijuana mellows out with age. The aging process tends to remove the chlorophyll taste.

10 MOST COMMON MISTAKES

Growing marijuana is not easy. It takes years of practice to be able to grow a potent sticky bud. However there are some common mistakes that majority of rookie as well as some experienced cannabis growers still make. Here a list of 10 common growing marijuana mistakes and advise how to avoid them.

1. Touch/Kill Germinating Seeds

Please have some patience. It sometimes takes 10 days for a seed to sprout. The paper towel method is not recommended because you must handle the seeds when transferring them from the paper towel to your growing medium.

2. Don't Over Water Your Marijuana Plant

Over watering kills marijuana plants. Water once the top few inches of the soil dry out. Hydroponics is harder to over water because rockwool has such excellent drainage properties. As long as the rockwool cubes are not sitting in liquid it is virtually impossible to over water a hydroponic setup. A hydroponic setup could either be watered constantly as the drip method, or once to three times a day as in the flood and drain method.

3. Don't Tell People You Grow Weed.

Seriously. Just don't. Why? They will only be jealous. People love to feel important and that is why they will tell other people; because others will listen to them. Keep it to yourself. This is one of the most common reasons for being caught, so again – don't tell anyone!

Daan Joie |

4. Don't Under Fertilize

Under fertilizing is less common but it happens. If you are one of those people that likes to give the plant just enough nutrients make sure you use a organic soil mixture with blood meal and bone meal or some slow release fertilizer with micro nutrients.

5. Grow Seeds From Seeded Marijuana

One of the greatest disappointments known to the growing man. 90% of what the final product will be is in the seed's genetics and has little to do with the environment the plant is grown in. Many get their hands on the seed and think they have a gold mine. They will probably grow something like this: hermaphrodites, tall late flowering females coupled with early flowering males. This is because the only pollen that could have produced the seed was from a hermaphrodite or a very stunted and late flowering male the grower did not notice. Unless you are prepared for possible disappointment don't use "unknown" seeds. This is why people buy seeds from seedbanks.

6. Don't Over Fertilize

Fertilize after first 2 spiked leaves appear. Follow the label. DON'T FERTILIZE EVERY TIME YOU WATER!!! Start with 25% and work your way up! Leach the plants with lots of pure water every 2-4 weeks. Organic marijuana growing is recommended. It tastes better and burns much better. If the leaves suddenly twist or fold under, Leach and Spray with pure water for several days!

7. Don't Harvest Too Early

I know it's hard. You see the buds and resin forming at a rapid rate. The buds are potent and you feel tempted to chop'em down! The only problem is that another 25% of the weight will form in 2 more weeks. Wait until the plants have totally stopped growing and the white pistils are at least 50-75% brown. *NOTE: Outdoors if security is a factor make your own call on when to sacrifice the fields. Also take buds continuously in case of thieves

8. Don't Start With Clones

Start with seeds. Bugs are a pain, So are plant diseases. Many growers are able to grow indoors without pest problems for years. If they do get pests they are probably not enjoying the change from their usual diet to marijuana resin! But as soon as you come in contact with others grow material (cuttings) it is almost guaranteed that its from a long time grower that has many different pests all eating marijuana and bug spray (and surviving) for hundreds of generations!... Think about it.

9. Don't Start Too Early Inside or Outdoors

For several reasons! If you are starting outdoors June 1 is perfect. But if I start earlier I will get bigger buds right? Probably Wrong!

It's strange but usually true. Let me explain. Plants started in early spring will get big but they will take significantly longer to start flowering. This is because at the peak vegetative period they sense the light cycles getting longer and longer, until June 21. But they don't realize that its time to flower yet. Finally in the middle of August the plant says "HEY, time to flower already" and it produces buds in August and September or later they will be tall as trees but thinner buds due to the fact that the sun is not as strong in September. Now if the ganja plants were put out later, as soon as they get a foot off the ground they say "what's going on" I am just in early veggie and the light hours aren't getting longer in fact SHORTER". Then the plants go crazy and since the sun is so bright in July and August you get amazing 6 foot trees that are heavier than the plants started in April!!! In addition to finishing earlier the late started plants are not nearly as noticeable.

Indoors is the same for different reasons. The light cannot penetrate more than a foot or two. So flower when plants are a foot tall. If you wait longer because you want bigger yields, you will get smaller yields and wait longer for them.

10. Don't Provide A Bad Environment

Always provide air circulation and fresh air even during the night cycle is fine. All the air indoors should be replaced every 5-10 minutes. Humidity between 30-70% temp aim for around 75-85' Even seedlings need a gentle fan to strengthen the stems.

How to tell male & female cannabis plants

The gender of a cannabis plant can be determined throughout its life cycle. The stages tend to be short in duration, so determining the difference at the optimal time is sometimes challenging.

Distinguishing the sex of a cannabis plant is often crucial to successful propagation and cultivation of the species because breeding both genders in close proximity can cause the whole crop to go to seed too quickly, preventing the harvest of intermediate axillary buds of the plant. It is important to determine the male and female plants so that they can be separated at the right times for the purpose of cultivation. Watching the whole cycle of a crop of cannabis helps you to distinguish the gender at each of these stages for identification with the next crop.

Note the pattern of leaf distribution in each plant of the crop. The plant grows up to 40 inches high, starting from its seedling or clone and then developing successive nodes on the initial stalk. The first indication of sex is visible when the leaves begin to sprout at these nodes. Female plants have significantly more branching and leaf growth than their male counterparts, which display only a few leaves in a seemingly random pattern. Determining the plant's gender at this early stage in the reproductive process allows you to separate male from female plants and ensure that the crop does not go to seed.

Note the shape of the flowers when they bloom. This is the stage in which the gender difference is most clear. Male plants develop tight clusters of ball-shaped flowers, whereas female plants produce V-shaped pistols that are covered in patches of fine white hairs.

Watch the behavior of the plants after they flower. Both of male and female plants look very similar until after they produce their flower. At this stage, the male plants have successfully engaged in their reproductive capabilities, tend to turn yellow and eventually die. Before they start to change color, the male plants can be harvested for their fiber. The female plants, in contrast, remain green for about a month after they produce their flower; this is the time when the seed ripens.

THE BASIC FACTS ABOUT MARIJUANA

Marijuana is notorious for being the world's most commonly used illicit drug. With nearly 200 names, marijuana is collectively known as pot, grass or weed. While the general population may believe weed is relatively harmless, it is far more dangerous than most users realize. Originating from the plant Cannibis sativa, the main mind altering (psychoactive) ingredient in marijuana is THC (delta-9-tetrahydrocannabinol), but more than 400 other chemicals can be found in the plant.

The strength of the drug and its effects, all hinge around the amount of THC that is in the weed. The strength will vary based on the type of plant, the soil, the weather, the time of harvest and other factors as well. Today's marijuana is about ten times stronger than the marijuana that was available to users in the early 1970's. The sophisticated cannabis cultivation of today reaps a much higher level of THC content, averaging less than 1 percent in 1974 and rising to an average of 4 percent in 1994. An increase in physical and mental awareness, due to a higher potency of THC, poses the possibility of health problems for the user.

Daan Joie |

How Long Do Chemicals from Marijuana Stay in the Body?

THC is absorbed by most tissues and organs in the body and can be primarily found in the fat tissues in the liver, lungs and testes. The body recognizes THC as a foreign substance and attempts to rid itself of the chemical, forming metabolites. Urine tests can detect THC metabolites for up to a week after users have smoked weed. Traces may be picked up by sensitive blood tests anywhere from two to four weeks later.

How is Marijuana Used?

Marijuana and other products derived from cannabis are usually smoked, either in a pipe or a water pipe. However, the majority of users will loosely roll a cigarette known as a "joint." Some users will take the time to hallow out a cigar and replace the tobacco with marijuana, to make what are called "blunts." Unfortunately, both blunts and joints can be laced with other substances, including crack cocaine or PCP, a very potent hallucinogen. This causes the user to experience a substantially mind altering high.

While smoking may be the primary choice for users, it certainly isn't the only route. Marijuana can also be brewed as tea or mixed into baked products such as cookies or brownies.

What are the Immediate Effects of Smoking Marijuana?

While some may argue this point, marijuana is considered to be a mild hallucinogen. An increase in pulse rate, faster heartbeat, bloodshot eyes and a dry mouth and throat are all symptoms that occur immediately. Studies have shown the drug can impair or reduce short term memory, alter a person's sense of time and reduce the ability to do things which require concentration, swift reactions, and coordination. Driving a car or operating machinery are not advised and may result in some serious legal slaps for those who choose to risk it. Moderate doses of weed will induce a sense of well-being and a dreamy state of relaxation.

"Acute panic anxiety reaction" is a fairly common adverse reaction that may be experienced by some users. A feeling of extreme loss of control can be overwhelming, causing panic rooted in fear. Fortunately, the symptoms usually disappear in a few hours.

Generally, users will feel the effects of smoking within a few minutes, with their high peaking in 10 - 30 minutes.

How Does Marijuana Effect the Human Reproductive System?

Studies have shown both men and women to have a temporary loss of fertility. Some research indicates that the use of marijuana during pregnancy may result in low birth weight and premature babies. During adolescence, our young people are experiencing rapid physical and sexual development, making it even more harmful during this time in their lives.

Does Marijuana Affect the Lungs?

Marijuana users often inhale the unfiltered smoke and hold it deep in their lungs for as long as possible, bringing the smoke in direct contact with the lung tissue for long periods of time. Not only does this irritate the lungs and damage the way they work, it also exposes the lungs to some of the same cancer causing ingredients found in tobacco smoke. Cellular changes known as metaplasia are considered to be precancerous and can be found in human lung tissue upon examination of those who have used marijuana for several years. The tars from marijuana have produced tumors when applied to the skin of an animal and it is suggested that it is likely to cause cancer in humans as well.

What are the Dangers for Young People?

Research shows that teens are more likely to experiment with other drugs based on how early they began using marijuana. They will often times lose interest in their schoolwork, becoming less motivated to complete the task at hand. Learning can become greatly impaired, effecting the ability to think, comprehend both in reading and verbal skills as well as mathematical skills being stifled. Research has shown that students are not capable of remembering what they have learned when they are "high". There seems to be a failure to master certain vital interpersonal coping skills. Ultimately, our young people who smoke weed set themselves up for the inability to make appropriate life-style choices and inhibit their own maturity.

Marijuana has been deemed as a "gateway drug", opening the door for the individual to explore more potent and disabling substances. The Center for Addiction and Substance Abuse at Columbia University found young people who smoke weed 85 times more likely to use cocaine in comparison to those in the peer group who chose to abstain from using. Additionally, 60 percent of our younger generation who have used weed prior to turning 15, later go on to use cocaine.

Marijuana Dangers

Increased Heart Rate

Anxiety, Panic Attacks and Paranoia

Hallucinations

Loss of Motivation

Increased Risk of Accidents

Impaired Judgement

Impaired Perception

Diminished Short-Term Memory

Loss of Concentration and Coordination

Diminished Inhibitions

Hallucinations

Psychological Dependency

Increased Risk of Cancer

Damage to the Respiratory, Reproductive and Immune Systems

If you or a loved one is struggling with marijuana use, please seek the professional advice of those in the field of drug and alcohol addiction.

Sabrina Coffin is proud to be part of a wonderful team of people who seek to help those who struggle with drug and alcohol addiction. Free by the Sea is located on a beautiful 5 acre campus, providing a serene healing environment that inspires patients to discover new possibilities for a life of recovery. The first 30 days of treatment includes individual treatment plans based on the needs of the client and addresses disease and recovery education, relapse prevention, anger management, emotion regulation, art therapy, meditation, 12 step meetings, life skills, transition and integration.

An extended care program is offered to patients who have stayed a minimum of 30 days. This allows for a continued focus on his/her relapse prevention needs and deeper issues to improve their quality of life, providing an even greater opportunity for success after completing our program.

WHAT MAKES MARIJUANA SO ADDICTIVE?

Many people debate over whether or not marijuana addiction is possible. While this topic may be commonly debated, the truth is not really up for discussion. The truth is that marijuana is addictive. In fact, it is estimated that one in ten people that try marijuana will become addicted. In fact, many people enter marijuana treatment programs specifically to treat their addiction to this drug. Let's look at marijuana a little deeper to determine just what makes this drug so addictive.

A good way to determine if something is addictive is to see how it makes people behave. People who suffer from marijuana addiction generally smoke it on a daily basis. On many occasions, the drug can interfere with jobs and school. Addicts often spend a great of time using marijuana, talking about marijuana and buying marijuana. This behavior is common amongst marijuana users, and some even find that they have to enter marijuana rehab to break the addiction.

Since marijuana changes how people see and deal with reality, oftentimes it can make daily life difficult. Rather than learning to process stress and frustration in a healthy way, addicts will reach for the drug. Over time, the marijuana use becomes far more than just a habit and it turns into a full-blow addiction.

The main chemical in marijuana that causes a feeling of high is called THC. THC travels through the lungs into the brain where it binds to certain receptors. This effect provides the feeling of being high. The short term effects of marijuana are forgetfulness, changed perception, coordination issues, time and space issues, to name just a few. Long term use can result in marijuana addiction and accompanying withdrawal symptoms that include irritability, anxiety, stress and drug cravings.

Many people that are addicted to marijuana also are at an increased risk for addiction to other drugs. It is believed that 2/3 of daily marijuana users also used other drugs in the last 30 days. Many of these drugs are extremely addictive and can cause other serious long-term problems.

Generally, the withdrawal symptoms fade in only a couple of weeks. However the presence of these symptoms make it hard for long term marijuana users to quit. Ask yourself the following question to determine if you suffer from marijuana addiction. Do you feel a need to use the drug even though it is causing problems with your personal, professional or family life?

Obviously, the best path is to avoid marijuana in the first place before marijuana treatment becomes necessary. However, if you already suffer from a marijuana addiction, recovery is indeed possible. Marijuana rehab centers have a very high rate of success in freeing users from drug use. Some users do need marijuana treatment to quit and there is certainly nothing wrong with getting help. The important thing is to start making changes that benefit your life and the lives of those around you.

THE HIGHS AND LOWS OF MARIJUANA USE

Is Legalising Marijuana Playing With Fire?

When marijuana is available legally for patients with medical conditions there can be a number of benefits if certain conditions apply: If the pharmaceutical drug options to relieve the patients symptoms carry more risks than marijuana; if the marijuana offers more therapeutic benefits than the pharmaceutical drugs and if the profits from marijuana sales are channelled into constructive enterprises that will benefit society as a whole.

Daan Joie |

However, legalising marijuana for recreational use is a whole different concept and one that has many people worried. The parties that are lobbying to legalise marijuana claim that legalisation will supposedly take the manufacturing and sale of marijuana out of the hands of drug addicts, drug cartels and other clandestine factions and into the domain of regulated manufacturers and retailers. Apparently, this will allow the taxes from sales to be directed into the public health and education systems, which would be far better than the current situation where only drug dealers benefit financially.

But there are several downsides to legalising marijuana for recreational purposes. One of the main issues is that legalisation sends out a message to impressionable adolescents that marijuana is perfectly acceptable. The other issue is that it will become far easier for minors to purchase marijuana even though it will supposedly only be available to those over 21 yo. Just like alcohol, teens can always find older siblings or friends to buy cannabis for them but having said that, it's already fairly easy for young people to purchase marijuana, whether it's legally acquired or not.

So What's Wrong With Marijuana?

Besides the statistics indicating that marijuana is a gateway drug for heavier drugs, marijuana itself can be very damaging to both physical and mental health. Physically it causes fatigue and increases the risk of heart disease and cancer, particularly lung cancer (if it's smoked) and cancer of the lymphatic system as well as oral tumours and other forms of cancer. Studies have shown that smoking marijuana is far more carcinogenic than nicotine and most people are well aware of the cancer risk from smoking cigarettes. Neurologically, marijuana is a well-known trigger for mental illnesses such as bipolar and schizophrenia and the damage it can cause to a developing brain can be catastrophic.

In normal brain development, significant changes occur in brain structure and function during the adolescent years and healthy brain function and growth needs to be supported via a healthy diet, ade□uate sleep and other favourable lifestyle factors. So consider the outcome if the developing brain doesn't receive the ideal requirements for normal growth and instead is exposed to neurologically-toxic substances such as marijuana (or other drugs).

Research carried out at the Northwestern University Feinberg School of Medicine in the US showed that adolescents who use cannabis regularly have abnormal changes to their brain structure and the younger the person is when they begin using marijuana, the greater the brain abnormality. Some of the brain damage that has been identified includes changes to the working memory - even two years after stopping the drug.

Furthermore, other research has shown that addiction develops very quickly, particularly in teenagers, and often results in the young person losing their motivation to engage in learning; no longer visualising and working towards their dream career and no longer caring about their health. The long-term risks of marijuana use are well-known such as cancer; mental health conditions and other risk factors - often resulting in regular users becoming walking zombies that are mainly focussed on their drug use and little else. Teenagers that are addicted to cannabis are also more likely to experience feelings of anger or discontent whenever they haven't had the drug for a while and therefore are at high risk of becoming anti-social and losing their friends.

The reason that addiction happens so quickly nowadays compared to years gone by is because the drug is so much stronger. So, these days, teenagers that begin smoking marijuana at parties may soon begin to smoke every week and before they know it, they are seeking it daily. Large numbers of addicted teenagers are smoking marijuana several times a day just to feel 'normal'. This sort of use has a dramatic effect on their developing brain; their heart and lungs; their ability to learn and on their finances - they either need to steal to pay for their addiction or they find themselves going to work just to pay for their habit.

Sadly, even those that decide to stop using cannabis are unable to repair the irreversible brain damage that may have occurred if they have been regular users during the critical brain development phase. Psychiatrist, Dr Paula Riggs, quoted the statistics from long-term research in New Zealand that was conducted on adolescents that regularly smoked marijuana. The research was carried out over 38 years and found that there was a 6-8 point reduction in IQ in regular users which can affect them for the rest of their lives. The brain damage caused by marijuana use includes a reduction in executive functioning which is an important set of mental processes that are required for organization, planning, memory and other essential brain functions. Executive functioning helps you to 'join the dots' in terms of what you have learnt in the past and how it relates to your current situation and what you need to do.

Therefore, regular use of marijuana alters the brain circuits in a really negative way and you don't have to be a rocket scientist to understand the impact this would have on brain development and the ability to achieve in life. As marijuana shapes the way the brain develops - a developing brain that is focussed on learning versus a brain exposed to mind-altering drugs may have dire conse◻uences for the rest of that person's life - even if they stop smoking marijuana later on. This is probably why the research shows that regular use of marijuana during the teenage years increases the likelihood of unemployment in adulthood or at best, results in a cannabis user or ex-cannabis user only being able to find work in (unsatisfying) sub-standard jobs that are far removed from the dream job they once saw themselves doing.

The only people to benefit from any kind of drug addiction are those that are making profits from the sales and I think it's a great tragedy that any government can 'approve' any substance that can irreversibly damage our young people's brains and potentially destroy their futures - no matter how much they may earn from the taxes on marijuana sales. Adolescents are vulnerable as the 'pleasure-seeking' part of their brain develops much faster than the 'self-control' part - leaving them much more susceptible to drug taking and other risky behaviours and they don't have the capacity to comprehend long-term consequences. Therefore, in my opinion, it's deplorable that a government doesn't protect their young citizens by saying "No" to legalisation.

Particularly as some of the legalised edible marijuana is being packaged specifically to appear like lollies which would be far more attractive to children and teens! So, call me cynical but it would appear that the marketing of marijuana is actually targeting our youngsters. This is despite the fact that eating marijuana allows much more THC to be absorbed into the body compared to smoking, so it increases the likelihood of overdoses, particularly in young people.

Parents, educators and policy makers around the world have a responsibility to protect our younger generations and should not be fooled by well-oiled marketing campaigns financed by those who stand to make millions while teenager's brain structures are being destroyed along with their futures.

If you are addicted to marijuana or have a family member that is, consult a ualified Counsellor that specialises in drug addiction as well as a Naturopathic Physician that is trained in substance abuse. There are a range of safe and effective natural medicines that are specifically designed to balance the neurotransmitters in the brain which can help reduce or eliminate the craving behaviour.

MARIJUANA

ADDICTION

SYMPTOMS

TREATMENT

Marijuana, cannabis, chronic, dope, ganja, grass, mary jane, pot or whatever people may call it, is a non-synthetic substance that comes from the plant cannabis sativa and cannabis indica. Its colors and characteristics vary depending where it is grown but its common hue is green. In the late 1800s the use and sale of Marijuana were regulated by a number of states and local governments in America. In 1906, several states controlled the drug by labeling it as a poison. By the 1920s, prohibition of the drug was entered in the constitution, and it was then repealed in the 1930s. Ever since, marijuana use continued to be illegal in the United States.

The marijuana plant is intended as a psychoactive drug. Our ancestors use them as a recreational drug and they use it for religious rituals as well. The use of marijuana is comparable to any other addictions such as alcohol abuse, cigarette, heroin and other drug exploitations. They have negative effects on man's health. Common side effects includes memory loss, slow learning, lack of concentration, loss of coordination, paranoia, emotional instabilities, poor perception or judgment.

Many people who are addicted to marijuana are hooked to its psychoactive effects due to the substance called THC or delta-9-tetrahydrocannabinol, which is the primary active component of marijuana. This substance is known to have a stimulant, depressant or hallucinogen effect. THC allows the brain to release its dopamine, a substance commonly known as pleasure chemical, giving the user a euphoric high. Euphoric sense is the main reason why people are getting hooked-up with marijuana.

Marijuana addiction is considered as a disease in many societies. Several groups considered marijuana users as outcasts. Thus, it lowers their confidence and morale towards self. Symptoms of addiction are loss of control over the drug and helplessness to quit regardless of the efforts exerted. Alongside with these symptoms, a strong urge of smoking marijuana is very common to the marijuana addicts. Whenever they failed to smoke, they feel depressed, anxious, unable to focus on other things and easily get angered.

According to research, treating marijuana addiction is not easy. Experts believe that there are no distinct medication to treat this kind of addiction. Treatment is the combination of detoxification, awareness on the bad effects of marijuana to the body, support of friends, families and loved-ones.

Detoxification - Experts believe that detoxification is the key therapy to treat chronic users of marijuana. Detoxification usually includes healthy diet, regular exercise, increase water intake and for some, detox pills. The detox program is directed at the physical effects of marijuana. Rehabilitation on the other hand, is a long-range goal so that the abuser will be completely free of the substance. The target of the program is lifestyle modifications.

Awareness - Many users are unaware of the bad effects of the marijuana to their physical, psychological and social being. Gaining knowledge on the harmful effects of marijuana can help chronic users to abstain from marijuana.

Moral support - As mentioned earlier, one reason why chronic users are having difficulty of quitting the drug and why relapses occur, is the lack of support from the people that surround them. Users need understanding, love, patience and special attention. Understanding will greatly help them in quitting the drug.

Marijuana addiction truly affects many people in different walks of life. Though marijuana use is illegal in the United States, it continues to be the most abused illicit drug in the most powerful country in the world. Aside from America, marijuana has been banned in many countries because of its various negative effects on man. In spite the prohibition, the abusers continue to grow. It is significant not to eliminate the importance of information dissemination about marijuana and other drugs so that people will not have to use it out of curiosity.

THE BENEFITS OF MEDICAL MARIJUANA

Studies have shown that medical marijuana can work well as a pain killer and anti-emetic (anti-nausea). It also helps to induce appetite. These qualities are helpful for patients suffering from cancer, especially after getting chemotherapy. These qualities can also help AIDS patients. Drugs that treat AIDS have side effects, and medical marijuana is effective in taking the edge off of them.

Specifically, THC may help patients who suffer from glaucoma. Studies show that it lowers intraocular pressure, thus giving a small bit of relief to those who suffer from the disease. It may also help folks who suffer from multiple sclerosis.

It relieves pain and treats spasticity, and the latest trials show that it may help in preventing the neurodegeneration associated with the disease.

THE BASICS OF

MEDICAL

MARIJUANA

The debate on the use of medical marijuana in the United States has long been ended. In fact, marijuana now can be purchased legally within 23 states of the US. It is also legal for marijuana to be used for recreational purpose in the states of Washington and Colorado. It goes to show that the medicinal value that is attached to the use of marijuana far outweighs any negative effects that comes along with its use. However, not everybody is convinced that medical marijuana is a good thing. There are now other countries such as

Australia that are debating on the legalization of marijuana use. Here are some of their arguments.

Pros. As early as 2737 B.C., marijuana has been used for treating gout, malaria and rheumatism in China. The use of marijuana spread throughout Asia until it reaches India where it was used for pain and stress relief. The medical use of marijuana soon got the attention of US and European countries.

Marijuana for medical use can be taken in several forms such as smoking, vaporizing and ingestion. There are 60 active ingredients called cannabinoids found in marijuana that are associated to its medicinal capabilities. Our body naturally produces cannabinoids that are responsible for modulating the amount of pain that our body is feeling. The main cannabinoid found in marijuana is the THC which is short for tetrahydrocannabinol. This THC triggers the CB1 receptors found in the brain, the nervous system, and other primary organs of our body. When the CB1 receptors are activated, they release hormones that will □uell stress and pain caused by damaged tissues or nerve cells. Studies have also revealed that medical marijuana reduces muscle spasms and other symptoms related to muscles becoming stiff.

Another medicinal use of marijuana is for stimulating the appetites of patients that suffer from suppressed appetites because of their medical conditions or treatment. Medical marijuana is prescribed to patients that are undergoing chemotherapy since this treatment will most often reduce a patient's appetite.

Although marijuana has been proven to have a lot of medicinal benefits, it goes without saying that its use may lead to different side effects. The THC of marijuana may affect the thinking and reasoning skills of its users. A person who is being treated with medical marijuana may have altered attention and judgement capabilities.

In the US, marijuana as a medicinal treatment is only being 'recommended' by doctors since the US federal law still prohibits the 'prescribing' of marijuana. Nevertheless, a person who wishes to purchase medical marijuana needs to have a diagnosis from a physician who will recommend the use of medical marijuana as a treatment for whatever illness they have.

Marijuana for medical use has been proven to be effective. However, like any other product, the abusive use of the substance can be detrimental to a person's health. The use of medical marijuana in other countries will rely on a country's belief system. Nevertheless, the use of medical marijuana must be strongly regulated.

BONUS

AMSTERDAM COFFEESHOP TOUR

Start: Amsterdam Centraal

1. Pink Floyd Coffeeshop

Adress: *Haarlemmerstraat 44, 1013 ES Amsterdam*

Very friendly stuff with good weed menu. This is a very popular place for tourists with good Pink Floyd music.

2. Hill Street Blues Market

Adress: *Nieuwmarkt 16, 1012 CR Amsterdam*

It's nice little coffee shop with a beautiful terrace and also comfortable inside room for smoking.

3. Abraxas Coffeeshop

Adress: *Jonge Roelenstg 12 -14, 1012 PL Amsterdam*

This coffee shop has a natural hippy feeling. Colorful mosaics and loud music make a great atmosphere.

4. Bluebird Coffeeshop

Adress: *Sint Antoniesbreestraat 71, 1011 HB Amsterdam*

One of the really busy coffee shops here in the Amsterdam so if you want to have a place better come early!

5. The Bulldog Coffeeshop

Adress: *Leidseplein 17, 1017 PS Amsterdam*

Bulldog bar and coffee shop is one of the first coffee shops here in the Amsterdam and it's also very famous. This is definitely must go!

End: Amsterdam Centraal

ONE MORE BONUS FOR YOU!

AMSTERDAM TOURS

When visiting this great European city for the first time, planning a route may seem overwhelming. Even with Amsterdam tours from a local expert, it can still be difficult to organize your time and see everything you'd like to see. In addition, you may miss some of the highlights just because you haven't heard about them, and your guide happened not to cover them. By being aware of key things to see before you leave home, you'll ensure that you get your pick of tours in Amsterdam and enjoy your trip as much as possible.

MUST SEE ATTRACTIONS

Don't Miss The Museums

Amsterdam tours almost always highlight how many museums the city has. It is host to numerous world-famous galleries, many of them dedicated to famous Dutch painters like Rembrandt, Van Gogh, and Vermeer. These galleries are a common stop on most touring routes, but if you're interested in a particular artist, you should ensure that the museum will be featured. In addition, look at a route that would take you inside the museum, or potentially a full tour of that museum.

Tours of Amsterdam Canals

The canal system is one of the most unique aspects of the city. There are boat rides available on the canals, but you can also explore them by walking alongside them. These canals were once used to ferry the nobles and merchants of old Holland, and almost every house alongside them was built specifically to appeal from the water. Geography and history students will be able to learn a lot from the way the canals have affected the city, while art-focused school groups should not miss the opportunity to get out the sketchbooks. A canal tour is also a fantastic way to get a feel for the city, so this is well worth including on the itinerary.

The Begjinhof Area

This area is one of the oldest in the entire city. It is something like a garden courtyard surrounded by very old houses, including No. 34, which has the honor of being the oldest house in the entire city. Once the home of a sect of nuns, the area is now open to visitors without restriction and many enjoy touring here. There is no entry fee, although many find it better to explore on guided excursions.

Magrere Brug Amsterdam Tours

This bridge is one of the most famous attractions in the city. It crosses the Amstel River, and is still in use today. As ships go underneath, visitors can witness the bridge lifting up just as it has done for more than a hundred years. Its construction is a highly traditional Dutch design, and it is almost a certain stop on most architectural Amsterdam tours.

The Anne Frank House

The story of Anne Frank is familiar to many visitors of the city. The home where Anne Frank hid during World War II is a fixture on many tours of Amsterdam, and also has exhibits inside of it. The entire Frank family lived inside a hidden annex of Anne's father's office building for two years, evading capture by the Nazis. They were

Daan Joie |

eventually betrayed, but Anne's diary survived. This site is a must see on any tours of Amsterdam, and is worth looking inside should you have time.

The Red Light District

Many visitors are surprised to learn that the Red Light District has some of the most spectacular traditional Dutch architecture in the city. It is one of the oldest sections as well. Although families may wish to skip this area simply because it is not preferred for minors even during the daytime, visitors who pass through here in daylight often find their trip enjoyable and very educational.

CONCLUSION

However, marijuana has its benefits as well as its disadvantages so you have to be careful when dealing with it, and when growing it necessary care should be given to the plant to make it grow well in the exact way you want.

Thank you for purchasing this book and finding the time out of no time to go through it please kindly read, assimilate the whole contents, and put them into implementation to get the best.

Thank you,

Daan Joie

36356224R00059

Made in the USA
San Bernardino, CA
21 July 2016